GIVERS
VERSUS
TAKERS

RUFUS RAWLS AND CAMERON FOX

STRATTON PRESS
We Celebrate Your Story

GIVERS VERSUS TAKERS
Copyright © 2022 **Rufus Rawls and Cameron Fox**

Stratton Press Publishing
831 N Tatnall Street Suite M #188,
Wilmington, DE 19801
www.stratton-press.com
1-888-323-7009

ISBN (Paperback): 978-1-64895-568-6
ISBN (Ebook): 978-1-64895-569-3

Printed in the United States of America

INTRODUCTION

Marriage is a sacred union, a mathematical contradiction where two equals one. It requires constant loving the same way the body requires a constant supply of oxygen, food, water, and rest. Keeping the flow of love constant and refilling its cup is an eternal commitment—a joint responsibility. Love must be fed and nurtured, and placing the needs of the partner equal to or greater than your own is most important. The table of commitment has to be set regularly, and making available a full-course meal of understanding is necessary to nurture love into maturity. A successful marriage is based on this premise.

The basic personality types are predominately GIVER and TAKER. The degree varies, depending on the unique background and experiences of the individuals. Conveniently included throughout this book, especially in chapter 5, "Speaking from the Heart," are personal ideas shared by energetic youths and adults. These candid and anonymous ideas lend insight into how our total concept of love, sex, and marriage helps to mold each individual into the GIVER or TAKER personality type.

THE GIVER

The GIVER understands that love needs constant loving and reassuring. This personality type has a natural ability to enjoy life and is able to share that unbridled joy. He or she exhibits an overflow of excitement about life. Ordinary events, viewed with love, become a production of caring and sharing. The attitude of the GIVER permeates all activities.

The five senses plus the intuitive sense are used to discover creative solutions to a problem. Unusual inner strength, introspective thinking, and the ability and willingness to communicate are second nature. The GIVER uses the "fruit of joy, peace, patience, kindness, goodness, faithfulness, gentleness" to include self-disclosure and commitment to strengthen the marriage or relationship.

GIVERS consult marriage counselors to learn new ways to reintroduce the concept of love into a failing marriage. They are open to suggestions and are not overly sensitive to criticism. GIVERS will gladly abandon old ideas and concepts that no longer enhance love. Sacrifice, though an old-fashioned word to many, is quite fashionable and welcomed by the GIVER. They relate well to the word, *now*, by putting untiring energy into the relationship as the need arises.

THE TAKER

The TAKER is often the selfish one, unwilling to let love grow and freely flow. Even when showered with love, the TAKER thinks, *This is not enough, I need more*, but *enough* is not easily defined. Due to a suspicious nature that prohibits the acceptance of love without question, the door to genuine love and affection is often tightly shut. Taking responsibility for his or her actions and feelings are habitually avoided. Questions concerning his or her role in the relationship create a sense of unrest, and a strong tidal wave of anger is stirred up in the subconscious. The TAKER fits Ralph Waldo Emerson's definition of someone who "runs in his own debt." He negatively uses his creative energy and often lacks the ability to rejuvenate. He often hides behind lies and deceit that invariably decreases his or her strength and stature. He thus reduces himself or herself to a size smaller than the lie that he or she is hiding behind.

The TAKER blames everyone for his or her problems except self. Yielding is very difficult. Marriage between two TAKERS resembles horses yoked together to a wagon with each determined to go in opposite directions. They have an insatiable need to be in control. If they were riding a horse together, their struggle for control would prevent the animal from maintaining a steady gait or a specific direction. There is little peace or compromise. It is a constant tug-of-war in which both lose. Two TAKERS pulling on the reins of what they perceive to be love will literally choke a marriage to death.

The TAKER uses many methods of torture. Very little inner joy is ever experienced. Frowns are part of their facial makeup, and a good sense of humor is a rarity. It is difficult to joke with a TAKER unless it is about someone else. Happiness is often equated with objects: money, cars, clothes, etc. Life is viewed as a devious game, and "getting even" is a favorite way of coping. Plotting continues in an overt or silent but consistent manner. The preservation of love is not considered. Individual victory is the theme and the motivation.

TAKERS consult marriage counselors to prove to the other that he or she is right. They often exhibit anger when not allowed to turn the session into a battlefield or shouting match. TAKERS are equipped with an arsenal of lethal weapons to do battle. Their defenses are practically impregnable. Word exchange between two TAKERS is very vicious. One will hurdle a negative word, and the other one will shoot right back. The discomfort level rises with each year of marriage. The battle continues without a winner but two losers. Once the battle is stalemated and both have exhausted their weaponry and themselves, divorce frequently follows.

Do GIVERS ever become TAKERS or vice versa? Sometimes, but it is often out of necessity. An illness or crisis can open up the TAKER's heart, but it is usually short-lived. The GIVER may also reverse roles during stressful periods, but because it is unnatural and awkward, it is usually short-lived also. However, TAKERS are not locked permanently into that personality type. In the words of Paul J. Meyer of Success Motivation Institute (SMI), "Before you can have, you must do. And before you can do, you must become." Change, starting from within the individual, can convert a TAKER into a GIVER. Negative change can have the same effect on a GIVER.

The differences between the GIVER and the TAKER lie in their ability to communicate with understanding and the degree in which they are willing to love. Remember the old tale about the two ducks swimming together one sunny afternoon. One looked at the other and said, "Don't go in front of me, I may not follow. Don't go behind me, I might not lead. Just stay beside me, and be my friend" (author unknown). Marriage does not require a leader, but two followers who can lead.

Part I

THE PROBLEM

PRELUDE
TO PART I

Marriage or any quality relationship is, to paraphrase Paul J. Meyer of SMI, "a journey and not a destination." Never allow complacency or taking your spouse for granted to sabotage the relationship. Metamorphosis is the order of life. Couples who desire a utopian union must be willing to change. Growth pangs are part of change in a relationship where love is the head of the household. When love replaces selfishness, a transformation takes place. Once the heart of the TAKER is opened to love and understanding, he or she is capable of change. The TAKER, whose inner voice and desires have been "me" focused, moves toward a new goal of "us."

The TAKER's shortcomings are highlighted, not as negative criticism but rather to contrast them with the GIVER's qualities that everyone should aspire to duplicate. In the words of a famous Chinese philosopher, "The death of a moth is the birth of a butterfly." The butterfly represents innovative ideas as a catalyst to change the TAKER into a GIVER. Thus the death or the transformation of the TAKER is the birth of the GIVER.

The objective of this book is to encourage the TAKER to make the transition to that of a GIVER and to help a GIVER improve self. Keep in mind that the degree of benefit will depend on your willingness to change. The first important step is to recognize the need for change, and the second is to be willing to change.

CHAPTER 1

Sex and Lovemaking

I watched her face change persons right before my eyes. Both frightened and fascinated, I convinced myself that she was the woman to quench the thirst made thirstier by all the others.

—Rufus Rawls

The processes of having sex and lovemaking are not the same. The Merriam-Webster Dictionary describes sex "as sexual activity or intercourse while it describes lovemaking as courtship." Sex is a serious and very personal act that should not be taken lightly. Whether intentional or not, parents, teachers, and religious leaders reinforce its seriousness one way or the other. Even children reared by "liberal" parents are influenced by numerous taboos.

A strong *sex guilt code* is implanted in our brain at an early age, and its presence is often ignored or overlooked until an attempt to break it is made. The code is often responsible for our unwillingness to explore and experiment with one another. It creates an uncomfortable presence, like a stranger watching while a couple engages in some form of intimacy. Guilt is, of course, a useful emotion, but it should not become a constant liability that stifles the relationship.

People who feel guilty tend to punish themselves and others with their very presence and attitude. A feeling of unworthiness prevents them from fully participating in the joyous aspects of life. Negative feelings become a part of them. An individual feeling guilty over past sexual activity will often lash out at the partner. The hidden anger from guilt is a strong barrier that can often hinder one from developing a genuine and loving relationship.

Lovemaking, not to be confused with sex, is the most intimate form of communication. It involves total communication that is important to the survival of the relationship as breathing is to the body. Just as a person will suffer brain damage and/or death if deprived of oxygen for more than several minutes, so too will a relationship die if there is prolong deprivation of communication.

The process of lovemaking involves much more than mere copulation. Both the rape victim and the rapist will have some twisted sort of sex, but neither will have experienced the intimacy and beauty of sharing love. Dogs, cows, and other animals all have sex. A prostitute will quickly explain that having sex and lovemaking are quite different. Lovemaking means to shed one's clothing, not only the outer garments, but also the fears and inhibitions that cripples intimacy. This release will enable partners to submerge themselves in love, freely sharing their feelings and expressing needs. Lovemaking is also wooing, tenderness, embracing, kissing, caressing, and fondling. It is a passionate love connection that touches the very center of the soul. When two people indulge in lovemaking, they are sharing the ultimate gift by becoming team players with the Creator of Life!

Lovemaking requires a willingness to commit to intimacy, to share without attempting to withhold part of self as a protective measure. Joy and pain are occasionally fraternal twins, but emotional vulnerability cannot be extracted from the pursuit of happiness. The thorns and the roses grow together.

When the love or marriage is new, the couple tends to wear their "Sunday faces," but over time, underlying pet peeves and personality idiosyncrasies will slowly surface when there is an intense concentration on each other's needs. As the relationship matures or with the passing of time, the qualities that were the focal point or the "alluring factor" becomes less and less obvious and may even fade into oblivion. It is at this point that one or both partners may become distracted and succumb to the "grass is greener on the other side of the fence" syndrome. The focus is now on the negative aspects of the spouse instead of the positive. Mark Twain stated this clearly in *Unpublished Diaries*: "Familiarity breeds contempt and children."

Lovemaking with couples committed to each other should be no less passionate than a beautiful work of art. Take a look at the great works of art and literature. None were conceived nor completed without passion! El Greco's oil painting of Toledo is an example of passion, as well as poems by Wordsworth and Shelley. "My heart leaps up when I behold a rainbow in the sky." "Life like a dome of many colored glass, Stains the white radiance of Eternity." What about Beethoven's Ninth Symphony or Gershwin's Rhapsody in Blue?

Infidelity is often a copout to avoid coping with the problems and challenges of a relationship. When talking to a stranger, we can choose to reveal only the information that will promote us to superhuman status. Chances are you have experienced sitting or waiting next to a stranger who revealed his entire life to you. Strangers find it easier to talk to other strangers. It is easier to discuss success or failure without fear of rejection, rebuttal, or reprisal. Strangers are good listeners and are willing to accept the individual in an unbiased manner. Also, what a stranger thinks is not as important as what a spouse thinks.

In marriage, it is impossible to permanently hide the negative aspects of the personality. They are there "the good, the bad, and the ugly" and cannot be successfully ignored.

Dr. David Viscott discusses guilt in his latest book, *Feelings*. "Severe guilt becomes a terrible trap.

If the guilty person begins to express anger, he may feel he's only proving he's the evil person he secretly suspects he is. They seem addicted to unfulfilling jobs and punishing life situations. The constant external torment at least spares them the burden of self-punishment. It is a tortured way to live."

The Secret

The secret to keeping a new car looking new is proper maintenance. Changing the oil on a regular basis, keeping it washed and waxed, and being careful to avoid potholes are but a few preventive maintenance procedures. Intimacy requires attention and "polishing."

But there are numerous saboteurs to lovemaking. Just as adding oil to a car's engine does not repair or overhaul the engine, cheating on your spouse will not repair or mend a broken relationship. Saboteurs present in various forms; the partner may become cold and aloof and stop saying the little sweet nothings that had previously been shared. Lovemaking should not be allowed to become a boring routine. Strive to remember music, poems, songs, places, and ideas that were once important. Allow spontaneity and anticipation to be an aphrodisiac. Although lovemaking cannot be maintained on a permanently high-intensity level, a more creative intensity should and can emerge.

Lovemaking is the summation of the total relationship. It is a process that involves the whole self—mind, body, and soul. It is a rare opportunity for partners to rise above the limitations and frustrations of daily life to a level of total unification.

Types of People

There are two kinds of people in the world: GIVERS and TAKERS. Each of us either gives to or takes from the relationship. TAKERS often view GIVERS as being weak pushovers who are either too submissive or unaware. TAKERS, to paraphrase John Milton in *Paradise Lost*, "believe that there are only two kinds of people in the world, the weak and the strong, and that the weak were put here to give pleasure to the strong."

Many individuals, through growth and maturity or the lack of, change from one to the other. A GIVER involved in a stillborn relationship may become overwhelmed by the lack of fulfillment and stoop to the level of the TAKER. However, the TAKER, with the help of a patient GIVER, is also capable of switching roles.

GIVERS strive to keep newness in lovemaking techniques by devoting time and patience. It is a joy for them to move forward into a deeper intimate behavior. They allow respect to grow and uniqueness to be discovered. The very thought of cheating is discomforting and will not be tolerated. They understand that the promiscuous are unable to truly love and are content to have a partner as a simple sex object.

Looking at the Giver and Taker

The TAKER often harbors negative emotions such as guilt, anger, fear, and jealousy, and hate is used as an emotional club to punish others as well as themselves. However, these emotions act as a boomerang and will return to the sender the fruits of the negative emotion in greater proportion. Emotions are not necessarily negative, but if selfishly used, they can damage the relationship and, in many cases, are the underlying reasons for health problems.

For example, the passing gear in your automobile is a very useful feature. It allows quick acceleration for passing and is convenient in other situations where speed is required. It is comforting and exhilarating to have at the bidding of your foot the available surge of power when you need to pass or avoid other motorcars. However, the passing gear in automobiles is only designed to engage for quick acceleration over a short distance. The engine is unable to sustain the constant pressure that the passing gear places on it. If it were to remain engaged for an indeterminate time period, damage to the engine is likely to occur.

Negative emotions have a similar effect on people. Truthfulness is a release valve that keeps pressure from building up. It is not easy for couples to lay things on the line, but it is an art that can be learned with openness.

A Final Word

If you keep on doing what you are doing you
will keep on getting what you are getting.
(Author Unknown)

Do not be deceived, God is not mocked, for
whatsoever a man soweth, that shall he also reap.
(Gal. 6:7)

Sex is the main emotional ingredient in love-making, but it alone unsupported by foreplay, tenderness, and a loving heart committed to sharing and caring is nothing more than an animalistic experience. In order to receive and to experience the joys that lovemaking includes, you must be a lover. If you decide to grow corn, for example, you naturally will have to plant corn seeds. If you want to harvest a large crop of corn, you have to plant the appropriate quantity of seeds. It does not take a clever farmer to understand this fact.

GIVERS are familiar with the above concept. They know instinctively that in order to reap joy, satisfaction, and bliss from a relationship, there must be a willing to give and to plant affectionate seed that will yield growth harmony. They understand the difference, and TAKERS who desire a well-rounded, reciprocal relationship are encouraged to approach intimacy as an art.

TAKERS seem surprised when they plant negative seeds and reap negative crops. An equally confusing habit of TAKERS is giving little and expecting much. TAKERS do not exercise a willingness to give without restraint. GIVERS give and receive in equal proportion and are blessed with generous dividends in return. The extent to which a relationship thrives or suffers depends on the type of individuals involved and their willingness to utilize the reaping and sowing concept.

WHILE LOVE IS GROUNDED BY OR ATTACHED TO DEEP EMOTIONAL FEELINGS, ITS VERY NATURE IS MUCH MORE. POETS AND WRITERS HAVE LABORED TO CAPTURE ITS SPLENDOR. MANKIND HAS CHASED ITS MYSTERIOUS PRESENCE ACROSS THE CONTINENTS OF TIME, DRIVEN BY AN UNENDING DESIRE TO POSSESS AND BE POSSESSED BY LOVE
(Rufus Rawls)

LOVE IS PATIENT, LOVE IS KIND, AND IS NOT JEASOUL; LOVE DOES NOT BRAG AND IS NOT ARROGANT, DOES NOT ACT UNBECOMINGLY; IT DOES NOT SEEK ITS OWN, IS NOT PROVOKED, DOES NOT TAKE INTO ACCOUNT A WRONG SUFFERED, DOES NOT REJOICE IN UNRIGHTEOUSNESS, BUT REJOICES WITH THE TRUTH;

BEARS ALL THINGS, BELIEVES ALL THINGS,
HOPES ALL THINGS, EDURES ALL THINGS.
(1 Cor. 13:4–7)

CHAPTER 2

What Is Love?

Several years ago, a nine-year-old child was discussing marriage with her dad. "An ideal husband," she said, "must be well educated, capable of earning a good living, and he should not leave his dirty underwear on the floor! He doesn't have to be really good-looking, but he shouldn't be ugly either." At the tender and innocent age of nine, she had obviously developed very definite ideas on the subject of marriage. More fascinating, however, is where did her philosophy come from at such an early age?

Concepts of love and marriage are shaped many times over as we grow and learn to communicate. Parents offer an early education on the subject from which the child listens, observes, and imitates. By the age of nine, for example, many of the biases and prejudices are firmly implanted. Impressions of the male and female roles, sexual attributes and handicaps, and social habits of both are set. Friends, teachers, and other significant role models serve as an extension of family by reinforcing or distorting ideas adopted from parents. Books, movies, ads, catchy slogans, and strong religious beliefs also influence views and have a definite impact on overall development. In fact, religion can either link love and marriage in a tender and caring or harsh and unyielding manner.

Since love is a learned endeavor, the individuals who appear to love freely are often those who were blessed with loving parents. They were exposed to a gentle form of love that carried with it a loving strength. Erich Fromm writes in his book, *The Art of Loving*, that any theory of love must begin with the theory of man and human existence. He describes the existential need for union between masculine and feminine poles.

Love, in its original, unpolluted form, is unconditional and amnesic. Love only requires love, and it is without negative memory. Any wrong committed against it is forgotten—discarded. Think of love as a lady or a gentleman who never brags nor boasts, and who does not retreat when faced with adversity.

You may ask, if love is so simple and clear-cut, why is the divorce rate so alarmingly high? In 1960, 393,000 divorces were granted in the United States. In 1980, that number had risen to 1,189,000. Is love now such an unloving power that the institution of marriage is becoming an "endangered species"? Love is certainly sought as much as food and debated as much as war and science. Its recognition as a powerful presence in the universe could clarify and eliminate many misconceptions.

Love requires giving unselfishly on a regular basis, and proper sustenance is required. The cup of love must not merely appear full but must be full. The only condition of love is that it is unconditional, a free-flowing essence that is both mystical and practical. The fringe benefits are for all to enjoy who are willing to embrace its essence.

The Ten Commandments of Love

1.   LOVE THYSELF.
2.   TRUST THY INSTINCTS.
3.   HAVE SOME OTHER GOD BEFORE HIM (not a self-worshipper).
4.   HOLD THY TONGUE.
5.   HEED WHAT YOU HEAR.
6.   KNOW THAT ACTIONS SPEAK LOUDER THAN WORDS.
7.   SEEK THE TRUTH BEHIND THE LINES.
8.   DON'T LET HIS LIGHT BLINDETH YOU.
9.   LOOK FOR THE MAN WHO HONORS HIS FATHER AND MOTHER.
10. DON'T BE QUICK TO BURN YOUR BRIDGES.

Pearl Buck writes, "LOVE CANNOT BE FORCED, LOVE CANNOT BE COAXED AND

TEASED. IT COMES OUT OF HEAVEN, UNASKED AND UNSOUGHT."

Love itself is not gullible to deception, although the individuals who seek it sometimes are. GIVERS intuitively realize that love is divine. Many TAKERS learn this in the course of living. It is like the sun shining on a joyful group of people. Each one receives its rays in their own manner, according to his or her awareness. The sun does not restrict its refulgent rays, and neither does it pick or choose who deserves its warmth because *it* just *is*. Although love is at the disposal of the worthy and unworthy, the best way to attract it is to recognize love and then become it.

Is love the only satisfactory answer to the problem of human existence? Can love be regarded as a way of life? Is it possible that it should be viewed as our holy destination? Can love be considered as the primary factor in solving the problems of relations rather than a secondary one? The questions are asked to provoke the love within you to seek the answers.

Whenever a relationship is confronted with anything negative or counterproductive, love should be viewed as both the patient and doctor. The partner who desires to do what is right as opposed to necessarily being right will invariable insulate the relationship by protecting the love with tender care and empathic understanding. When love is nurtured and allowed to grow without restraint or demand, every act by a couple will be blessed by their supreme goal of love. Actions will either strengthen or destroy the relationship. A decision not to permit love to thrive and blossom is a decision to let it wither. The decision is based on the degree of unity within the union and the philosophic importance of love.

A symbolic attachment does not reveal the true nature of love. If a person can only show his love to one person and no one else, it is an enlarged egotism. This person will often have great needs to control someone. Their philosophy of love is simply not grand enough to allow others to partake.

Love among the Givers and Takers

Love is a total concept and reality. TAKERS are frequently unaware of the gap in their personality. Love cannot be given to some and withdrawn from others. It is not something that can be divided. It is all or nothing! It is a matter of becoming fully aware of the essence of another person. "Love," according to psychiatrist and philosopher Viktor Frankl, "is the salvation of man."

GIVERS have a profound understanding of love. The TAKERS are vague and do not fully understand the enormity of the concept. These concepts are described in the book *The Givers and Takers* by Bruce Feld and Chris Evatt. They portray Givers as those persons able to get outside of themselves and became aware of others. Takers put more energy into their own subjective world. Givers feel joy in giving, and Takers feel joy when they are receiving.

One idea that is considered the standard by many is that love is a fifty-fifty proposition. To constantly expect this proposition to be adhered to will invariably restrain one while overburdening the other. TAKERS convince themselves that they deserve more than fifty-fifty, and often GIVERS somehow believe that they deserve less. The energy that flows back and forth from GIVER to TAKER should be a natural flow, therefore not always fitting into the fifty-fifty concepts. Love is to be shared without measurement.

LOVE IS NOT PRIMARILY A RELATIONSHIP TO A SPECIFIC PERSON, IT IS AN ATTITUDE, AN ORIENTATION OF CHARACTER WHICH DETERMINES THE RELATEDNESS OF A PERSON TO THE WORLD AS A WHOLE, NOT TOWARD AN OBJECT OF LOVE.
(Erich Fromm)

TAKERS find it difficult to develop the capacity to love completely and without ulterior motives. Their understanding is vague, and the concept is so enormous and overpowering that fear prevents them from exploring the joyous depths of love. A love that is a composite of maturity, self-knowledge, and courage can be scary for both the GIVER and TAKER. Learning to love, like other arts, demands practice and concentration. It also demands genuine insight and understanding.

The Responsibility of Husband and Wife

The inability of husband and wife to love each other inseparably does not have just a single consequence. The destruction of a sacred union that leaves family and children as causalities is reason enough for alarm. The breakdown in the family unit that culminates in divorce exposes the terminal phase of the problem that trickles into all areas of society. The problem spreads to neighborhoods, schools, communities, and ultimately nations.

To expect world peace when the family unit is being destroyed is a futile goal. Love, in order to become a more global reality, must originate and spread from the family nucleus. Love must be revived as a zealous pursuit, an art! It can no longer be regarded solely as a noble idea. Love on the individual level can grow and prosper on a larger scale. We have seen this happen with hate; why cannot the reverse take place? The time and need is right for love to become a priority goal that should be analyzed and approached with the same fervor as careers, sports, and investments.

A Final Word

The word *love* is diverse in that it means different things to different people, ranging from its purest form to being regarded as a philosophy or hobby. It has unique properties and qualities that are innately unique to each of us. The most demanding challenge is to reach deeply within self, open the arms of your heart, and allow love to grow by nurturing its total concept.

CHAPTER 3

Communication

The Perfect Marital Recipe

Relationships are as uniquely different as the individuals themselves. Thus, finding a single profile that clearly defines a happy and ideal marriage or relationship is difficult. Love and respect, honesty and kindness, and understanding and a sense of humor are basic qualities of marriage. While each is very important, communication is likened to the flour in the recipe of marriage. Without it, the quality of the union is substantially reduced and the probability of failure greatly increased.

One dictionary defines *communication* as "the imparting or interchange of thoughts, opinions or information by speech, writing or signs." Let's parallel the importance of communication in marriage to the importance of flour in a cake. Common ingredients in a cake—in addition to flour—are eggs, margarine or butter, baking powder, and flavor. The quality or taste of the cake is determined by the correct measurement of ingredients, and the ingredients vary depending on the kind of cake. Forget the flavor, and you still have a cake, not as tasty, but still a cake. If the baking powder or eggs are missing, it will not rise as much and will not be soft and fluffy but still a cake. If the flour is excluded, regardless of the other ingredients used, you will have a concoction that is something other than a cake! Obviously the flour or batter is the single most important ingredient in the cake. Although the others help to improve its taste, it is the flour or batter that makes a cake a cake.

In marriage, communication is likened to the flour, the single most important ingredient. Honesty and kindness are likened to the eggs, love and respect are the baking powder, the flavor is the understanding that resolves friction and indifference from the relationship, and a sense of humor is the icing on the cake.

The right marital ingredients, if you will, must be properly mixed and balanced. The secret is to fully utilize them and not forget the *little important things.* Just as every automobile has a blind spot, an area where other automobiles or objects are temporarily blocked from the driver's view, our personalities have similar blind spots. Although differences sometimes mean disagreement, they can allow a couple opportunities to shed light on each other's blind spots. While similarities create harmonious interaction, dissimilarities promote individualism as a natural area where growth is discovered. The results can strengthen the most vulnerable links, giving couples the necessary tools to tackle any marital problem with a common goal of victory.

A thriving relationship explores all beneficial possibilities. Effective communication means putting all the cards on the table, the entire deck, and reaching an acceptable solution.

Using Anger as a Communication Tool

Anger is a negative form of communication used by GIVERS and TAKERS. There are always unexpected situations that throw healthy interaction into a tailspin that brings out aggression. Even GIVERS married to GIVERS experience emotional upheavals. Usually the barrage of word slinging fails to resolve the original issue and creates a totally new set of problems.

The presence of anger is not necessarily expressed in an aggressive and clear manner. There is little difference between the chronically angry and aggressive person and the dependent angry person. The former's emotions are as explosive as nitroglycerin, while the latter's temperament is insidious and less obvious. Both communicate in an offhanded manner that leads nowhere. A dependent personality type is often reluctant to show anger out of fear of what it might do to the relationship. Will the love continue? Will it cause rejection? Will I continue to get my dependency needs met?

The passive and dependent person, who generally does not feel as good about self, harbors anger.

The dependency needs were created in the past but are nurtured in the present. The anger disguise has to be stripped of its protective coat. The pain of the past has to be brought to the NOW. It is common knowledge that many of the happiest people in the world tend to be independent. The knowledge of being in control is the foundation of that independence. They know that if placed on a deserted isle, they will survive. Being puppeteers of circumstances, under the richest conditions, some dependent individuals find survival difficult.

SO YOU WANT TO KNOW ABOUT ANGER—
ANGER DESTROYS PEACE, NEUTRALIZES
LOVE, ENGENDERS HATRED AND
TURNS INDIVIDUALS, NATIONS, AND
GROUPS INTO ENEMIES. THIS IS DONE
TO SATISFY A LOWER IMPULSE TOWARD
DESTRUCTION. IT IS THE OPPOSITE OF
LOVE. IT ALWAYS FALLS BACK ON THE
ONE THAT INDULGES IN IT. YOU CAN
RECOGNIZEE ANGER IN SLANDER, EVIL
GOSSIP, BACKBITTTING, FAULTFINDING,
PEEVISHNESS, IRRITABILITY, SURLINESS,
GROUCHINESS, JEALOUSY, MALICE,
IMPATIENCE, RESENTMENT, MALICIOUS
MOCKERY, DESTRUCTIVE CRITICISM,
AND HAUGHTINESS. THESE ARE
ALL OFFSPRINGS OF ANGER.
(Paul Twitchell)

Role Casting

If we think of ourselves as someone who always reacts in a certain manner, whether it is volatile or docile, chances are we will consistently react that way. Former president Ronald Reagan, for example, adopted the role of being cheerful years ago. He maintained that disposition through operations, crises, and constant changes. Even while on the operating table, he shared jokes with the attendants.

Role-play is used in therapy to assist couples to reverse roles. This provides insight into the other's role and lessens the judgmental stance. *Casting* ourselves in a different role has therapeutic benefit. Pretending for one day to be someone who calmly reacts to difficult situations will establish the fact that a more serene approach is possible.

Actors sometimes play a part so long until they actually adopt the characteristics of that person. Did not John Wayne *look and sound like a cowboy*? We are all actors. Shakespeare said that we all have our hour on the stage. Life is that hour!

GIVERS do not practice insulting each other with abusive language or negative deeds. Their choice of words is intended to encourage each other to take the next step necessary to improve communication, thus improving the relationship.

THE BEST WAY TO CHANGE ONE'S PERSPECTIVE OF THE PAST IS TO DEAL HONESTLY WITH THE FEELINGS OF

THE PRESENT AND TO RESOLVE THOSE
FEELINGS AS COMPLETELY AS POSSIBLE AS
THEY OCCUR. IF YOU ARE ANGRY, SHOW
IT. DON'T PRETEND YOU ARE ABOVE
SUCH FEELINGS. DON'T TRY TO IGNORE
THEM AND BURY THEM IN THE PAST.
(Adelaide Bry)

Joan and Jo are a perfect example of GIVERS working as a team. Joan did not want Jo to take a two-week hunting trip to Alaska. She knew it would be expensive and hated the idea of being left alone. She was also disappointed that he wanted to spend his vacation in Alaska rather than with her. Joan's first objective was to establish the importance of the trip to Jo. Was it important to his career, or just something he wanted to do? How would it affect him if he did not go? Jo was equally receptive to her point of view. Was it important to go on a vacation together? Was the trip to Alaska going to place a strain on the relationship that will linger after his return?

They sat down and discussed available options without suffering feelings of dread or fear. Mutual trust enabled them to weigh all the possibilities and emotions involved to make the best decision for the relationship.

The ultimate purpose of the conversation was to preserve the relationship. There was not a tug-of-war with out-of-control words or flying emotions, as is often the case with TAKERS. The negotiation process began immediately. They wanted each other to be content with the results. Jo took the trip to Alaska, but stayed only one week. The second week was saved for them to vacation later in the year. Joan got a friend who lived alone to stay with her. They attended plays and enjoyed other activities that Jo did not especially enjoy.

GIVERS exude a sense of harmony that can be felt even in a crowded room. As playful as children, they bring that spirit out of hiding for the entire world to see. They concentrate on communicating with every inch of their being, energizing one another with love. An understanding of mutual love creates an openness that is beyond ordinary forms of communication. GIVERS have problems just like everyone else, but they approach them hand-in-hand with tenacity and vigor that leads to victory. "*Do you know who is alive? The one who is born in love*" (author unknown).

GIVERS do not repress criticism. They welcome ideas different from their own as an opportunity to enhance individual growth and to preserve love. They are not afraid that the peaceful synchronous or in-sync relationship will be dissolved by it. They resemble professional ballroom dancers.

One could easily get the impression that this is a simple task. It only seems simple following hours of dedicated practice. This is not an automatic reaction to each other, but one that is practiced over and over until it is perfected.

Can couples practice and become efficient in moving together in a synchronous marriage? They certainly can! It takes dedication to love and the relationship.

The Reciprocal Benefit of Giving

Li and Chun have a GIVER-GIVER relationship. Lisa wanted to return to college to become a nurse. Chun was a pharmacist. With their children about to graduate high school, the family was financially secure. Lisa thought it was finally time to pursue a career she had delayed years to concentrate on the family.

One evening, Li shared her desire with Chun during their evening walk. He expressed a sincere interest and asked questions pertaining to the proposed course of study. He willingly agreed to help with homework and children's activities and made himself available to do whatever he could to make things easier. The discussion was not completely resolved, but time was set aside to discuss the issue further.

Li and Chun gave each other the respect deserved by listening and asking pertinent questions, honoring the importance of the subject, and allowing the conversation to flow. Although the issue and all the particulars were not immediately resolved, they went to bed knowing that because the relationship was the MOST IMPORTANT ISSUE, a mutually acceptable decision would be met.

The love of these GIVERS is genuine, the kind that grants freedom of expression. Their conversation was not tied in a knot by egotism. The TAKER, on the other hand, transmits messages that say, "You are not worthy of my love unless you act like I want you to act!"

The TAKER often picks apart his or her mate until there is no love left. The law of inertia in physics is the "tendency of matter to remain at rest if at rest, or, if moving, to keep moving in the same direction, unless affected by some outside force." The TAKER can be compared to someone stuck on a fast-moving treadmill, victimized by the law of inertia. Due to the effects of that law, getting off takes a surge of dedication and encouragement.

The following captures the friction in a relationship where TAKERS are involved:

Therapist: What brings you here today?

Male: My wife wants to improve our marriage.

Female: Yes, that's right. We need help, or I'm going to leave him.

Male: She's always threatening to leave.

Therapist: Can you tell me something about your marriage and how you spend your time?

Male: That's easy. I spend my time working and taking care of everything, and she spends hers not caring about nothing!

Female: That's simply not true. I work just like he does. He just happens to be obsessed with keeping everything perfect—I can't stand it anymore! He screams and fusses if there is even so much as a glass left in the sink.

Male: Everything does have its proper place.

Female: The world won't come to an end if something is not in its place.

In order to better understand the impact their roles were having on the relationship, the therapist talked with each individually. The couple mutually agreed that the wife would be seen first.

Female: He's impossible to enjoy. All he thinks about is working or cleaning. I feel as if I don't know him, and we've been married for a year. We never do anything just for the fun of it.

She went on to describe his obsessive behavior with vacuuming and dusting. He makes a detailed list of tasks to be done nightly and weekly. He was inconsiderate of her plans and insisted on dictating every activity with military precision.

Male: I can't stand a nasty house. She'd live in a pigpen if I didn't care. Her family is the very same way!

He ranted on and on, describing his preoccupation with perfectionism and trivial details. The tone of his voice was strong and angry, and his face was without expression. He admitted being under tremendous pressure at work, having to work overtime in order to get the job done "just right." He did not have any close friends and complained that his coworkers did sloppy work. It was apparent his compulsive personality prohibited him from leading a serene and happy life. Living with such compulsiveness, it was hard for his wife to be a GIVER.

The chronically anxious or depressed also experiences difficulty attempting to improve a relationship. The anxious person is irritable, impatient, and apprehensive most of the time. A depressed person is withdrawn and sad, not as mentally alert, and suffers a loss of interest in life. Communication skills can usually be improved, although the improvement is oftentimes short-lived.

Mary Lynn walked into the office and asked for "a few minutes." Her jersey dress fit so tightly that it crawled up her thighs when she sat down. With a shiny and garish made-up face, she cried and talked at the same time. Her conversation went from one extreme to the other as she walked back and forth from the window. One minute her voice was clear, and the next it was hysterical.

Mary Lynn is the TAKER in the family. In the course of a twenty-minute session, she used the phrase "I want" at least twenty times. She had an irrepressible need to be the center of attention, and when deprived the spotlight, she would become hysterical, like a spoiled child denied her favorite candy. Her appearance, actions, and dialogue supported this need for attention. Her unconscious cry was "Watch me, listen to me, and love me!" The histrionics were playing so loudly in her head that she would not allow Paul to penetrate her highly protected thought world.

Paul had become exhausted from trying to fulfill her every demand. He had cut back on his out-of-town business trips, quit bowling with the league at work, and had discontinued some church activities. This was not enough for her. Since he was sincerely committed to preserving the relationship, he was willing to try other suggestions. Whenever he talked to her, the tone of his voice echoed with love, and his body twitched with a desire to get closer to her. He began to show her attention when she least expected it. One morning he called to share with her a humorous story that had transpired at the office. One evening he surprised her with a dozen beautiful roses. Finally she began to notice the stress he was under.

The TAKER and GIVER relationship will never be easy, but Paul was determined to succeed and was willing to put love first. Mary Lynn realized her self-esteem had to improve in order not to need as much approval from Paul. He addressed her fear of insecurity with reassurance he would never abandon her. It took dedication and hard work to keep the marriage together. They were willing to make the sacrifices necessary to nurture the failing relationship back to health.

Drug and Alcohol Abuse

The use of drugs and alcohol has reached epidemic proportions. An extreme example of miscommunication or maladaptive synchrony is a relationship where one partner is an abuser of alcohol or drugs. The alcoholic often learns how to be very charming in order to get what he wants. Regardless of what he says or does, he has an ulterior motive incompatible with genuine love. He is emotionally blind to everyone's needs except his own. The addict's impaired social functioning cripples his ability and willingness to love.

Communication is improved by sharing new ideas and events. The addict's inability to be open and honest creates a severe imbalance. The healthy partner reacts in an unhealthy manner, and soon there is lack of balance in the marriage.

A Final Word

Communication is the vehicle that permits love to flow smoothly from individual to individual. A block in the flow invariably damages the relationship. Many relationships fail, not due to lack of love, but rather the lack of humility to communicate in a spirit of love and understanding. The preservation of love should be the ultimate objective in the relationship. Therefore, embrace love with open arms, seek its guidance at every opportunity, enjoy its presence on every occasion, and be thankful that although love is at constant war with the opposition, it is the most powerful force on the earth. Communication is the protective armor of love.

GIVERS VERSUS TAKERS

LIFE IS NOT MADE UP OF GREAT
SACRIFICES AND DUTIES, BUT
OF LITTLE THINGS, IN WHICH
SMILES AND KINDNESS AND SMALL
OBLIGATIONS, GIVEN HABITUALLY,
ARE WHAT WINS AND PRESERVES THE
HEART AND SECURE COMFORT.
(Humphrey Dave)

MANY COUPLES PLAY THE OLD MIND
READING GAME BUT THEY ARE NOT
EVEN GOOD AT IT. OFTEN ONE WILL
SAY THAT HE KNOWS WHAT THE OTHER
IS THINKING. THIS AUTOMATICALLY
PREVENTS A SMOOTH FLOW OF
CONVERSATION OR CREATIVE IDEAS.
COUPLES HAVE TO BE DISCOURAGED
FROM PLAYING THIS GAME.
(Leo Buscaglia from *Personhood*)

CHAPTER 4

The Beauty and Intimacy
of Communication

We communicate with the purpose of sharing an idea that is important to us. If what we value is discounted either by words or actions, communication is prematurely interrupted. This creates a void for the person with the idea. Love and intimacy require some verbal expression. It is a lover's responsibility to reach out and touch the heart of the loved one—a word, a note, a flower, or a simple poem can bring a much-needed message of assurance. It is a reckless habit to assume that the other person or persons know what we are thinking or how we are feeling. It is ironic that most individuals are surprised when this is found to be untrue.

Ignoring problems instead of attacking them with love and tenacity is a common mistake of married couples. Confrontation is avoided by bad feelings stored up like a squirrel storing nuts for the winter. These feelings are dragged out of storage at convenient times.

The Lion's Roar of Takers

The ego of a TAKER is like a hungry lion always roaring to be fed. THE *king of the beasts* never lets up or gives in. The chronic TAKER has an ego that reigns supreme over their actions and reactions. The TAKER spends time seeking victory rather than learning to understand self and others. The TAKER'S failures loom heavily and plagues communication without easy resolve. The mistakes of the past create a barrier that makes communication extremely difficult. The relationship can be severely threatened by these unresolved problems. The solution is to utilize as many options as possible. However, it is difficult to freely discuss the many available options when the ego is roaring and making untrue accusations. It screams, "*My way is the only way*," or "*I have to be right to prove myself*." The result creates division, and the couple becomes opposing foes. One TAKER may plot to devise an unscrupulous game plan to get whatever desired. The other automatically senses the confrontation and prepares to defend self. This type of relationship does not allow room for compassion or compromise. It is based on competition.

When interpersonal conflicts gain enough negative momentum to push love aside, the relationship can rarely be salvaged. These conflicts repeat again and again because the basic interaction is unbalanced and unloving. Once you have identified a deep lingering or interpersonal conflict, strong determination and a clear strategy are required. Generally, the inability to triumph over significant interpersonal conflicts will completely alter or *end* a relationship. If communication is sabotaged, growth and development are stifled. A communication crisis is as critical as a massive heart attack, and immediate love-aid is required to revive the relationship.

Attend any divorce proceeding, and observe the competitive spirit at its worst. If one roaring lion is not enough, there are two. A truce, of a sort, is met only after one party declares *victory*.

The Art of Negotiation

The importance of learning how to lovingly and agreeably disagree, to discuss an issue and reach a mutually agreeable solution, cannot be overemphasized. It is important to the nurturing of the relationship. Otherwise, it may become stalemated.

Larry and Susan are good examples: Larry wants to vacation at his favorite beach. Susan wants to go to the mountains. Unable to mutually agree, they fight a tug-of-war that leaves them exhausted.

The simple word, *understanding*, is not a tool used in their conversation. *I, I, I* is the predominate word used. A cloud of negative emotions soon forms around them like a thick blanket of fog. Searching and pushing for dominance prevents them from understanding why they desire different vacations. They became so engulfed in this cloud that the original argument is soon forgotten as anger lashes out like a serpent's tongue.

Do Not Attack Criticism

A wife talks to her husband in the kitchen as she prepares a dish. He casually remarks that she is using too many spices. Her ego did not accept his criticism objectively. It roars and rears its ugly head and demands that she accept his comment as a personal attack on her ability to cook. One without an oversized ego would simply have asked questions, laughed it off, or been grateful for the help. The TAKER's ego rejects criticism or what is perceived as criticism. Remember, the ego has to be fed constantly with agreement and approval.

The TAKER is refusing to listen—the loud roar of the ego is offended, hurt, or mad! This automatically places tremendous strain on a marriage. It is impossible to live with someone who expects total approval on everything. Love does not require, nor should total agreement be expected. Differences have magnetic properties that encourage growth.

TAKERS share a few precious moments of intimacy. Chances are you are wondering how two people completely wrapped up in their own demanding egos of philosophic selfishness can remotely express intimacy? Anger can be a form of intimacy, and the TAKER has plenty of it. Anger goes out and tantalizes the other until it gets a reaction. When the reaction is received, the anger is returned to the sender, and what you have is *bonding*. An anger bond is as strong as rope, as sticky as glue, as versatile as clay, and as certain to return as a boomerang! Yes, there is a great emotional bond in anger, and it will persist until it is broken. TAKERS do not yield very quickly, but prefer to show force to one another.

Food for Thought

Lao Tzu lived in China in the province of Hunan. A contemporary of Confucius, his philosophy known as Taoism was influential in developing Chinese thought and culture. He wrote about force and understanding the use of it and the opposite of it in his book, *Tao Te Ching*.

The softest thing in the universe
Overcomes the hardest thing in the universe
That without substance can enter where there
Is no room.
Hence I know the value of non-action.
Teaching without words and works
Without doing are understood by very few.

The preceding quote is very profound and can obviously be interpreted in many ways. One is that couples should learn to use both conversation and silence to communicate, learn the value of action and nonaction, and to ultimately learn that love will eventually defeat any adversary. Its time frame may differ from ours, but victory is inevitable!

Profile in Courage

Marriage is not normally regarded as a call to be courageous. Yet it is a courageous act to consciously treat each other with respect. A screaming couple addicted to name-calling came in for counseling. Both had many wonderful images of courageous people. He talked at length about John Kennedy, and she talked about General Patton, Gloria Steinem, and President Reagan.

When discussing their individual jobs, their faces lit up with joy and pride. The least discussion of themselves prompted squinted eyes and hostile voices. The challenge of not treating each other in a demeaning manner was selected as the supreme goal to salvage the marriage. Neither had specific qualities they disliked about each other. They had simply programmed themselves to treat each other in this manner.

As a part of therapy, they were encouraged to try something new that required courage. She took ice-skating lessons; he took violin lessons that also prepared him to accept a new and creative project at work. These new activities diverted attention away from previous stimulations—name-calling, screaming, and destroying each other's self-esteem.

They returned in two weeks and discussed the courage it took to accomplish the new goals. With enthusiastic voices, it was evident the challenge of the unknown had greatly improved their attitudes. The next step was to transfer those courageous feelings into the relationship. He was willing to be the first brave one and contracted with her to spend the next twenty-four hours without saying anything cutting or nasty. He succeeded by maintaining a strong association with the word *courage*. This was a start. She agreed to spend the next twenty-four hours with the same contract.

> To be courageous requires no exceptional qualifications, no magic formula, no special combination of time, place, and circumstances. It is an opportunity that sooner or later is presented to us all.
> (John F. Kennedy)

> Courage isn't a brilliant dash,
> A daring deed in a moment's flash;
> It isn't an instantaneous thing
> Born of despair with a sudden spring.
> But it's something deep in the soul of man
> That's working always to serve some plan.
> (Edgar A. Guest)

The desire to become a GIVER instead of a TAKER takes real courage. GIVERS have the courage to be grateful for the relationship. Gratitude can be demonstrated in a thousand ways, but improved communication techniques are vital. The TAKER can be encouraged to internalize the words *courage* and *gratitude*.

The Fruits of Education

We live in a highly sophisticated culture where a high premium is put on education. We are taught at an early age how to read, write, and how to grow up to be responsible adults in society, yet our knowledge of sex is proportionately low. It is difficult to get couples to understand the importance of sex education. This fact is evident in the following conversation between Stan and Therapist:

Stan: I've been having sex since I was eighteen, and Doris (wife) doesn't think that I know anything about it!

Therapist: Your information has been useful to you in the past. Maybe there's new information waiting for you now.

Stan: Like what?

Therapist: We could start with a chart of the female anatomy and just discuss that.

Stan: That sounds silly, but I'll do it.

The therapist placed a large chart of the female body in front of Stan. He agreed to name the parts of the body that had sexual significance. This simple exercise emphatically revealed how much he did *not* know.

Doris participated in the same exercise at another session and was equally ignorant about the male.

Doris: It's the man's job to please the woman.
Therapist: Can you tell me how he'd go about doing this?
Doris: Not exactly, but he should know.

Stan was pretending to understand Doris's sexual needs and sensitivities, and she was pretending to understand his. A healthy understanding of their erogenous zones aided this couple in experiencing intimacy and sensuality. Education was a good place to start bridging the gap of information. They begin to realize that education is vital to lovemaking.

The therapist emphasized the childlike playful approach. The seriousness Stan and Doris had used in the past was no longer working for them. With the help of their new knowledge, it was not long before they began to explore one another. They gradually discarded their inhibitions and developed a playful relationship that was more conducive to genuine lovemaking. Just observing them was similar to watching kittens at play—touching, backing away, getting close, kissing, purring, stroking, and interacting in sensuous ways enhanced their love.

Stan and Doris had a common problem often ignored until it causes a relationship to deteriorate beyond repair. The big three-letter word, *sex*, was separating rather than joining them. Stan, who had exhibited many of the TAKER's attitudes, became a GIVER in the area of their lives that helped to preserve the relationship.

The fear of pregnancy, loneliness, criticism, and poverty can all become strong barriers for couples to hurdle. The fear of passion is often observed in counseling sessions. If the personality needs control, as TAKERS often do, passion will be bridled and rationed.

Larry enjoyed many sexual encounters before marrying Ann. He was now ready to settle down in a monogamous relationship, but she was having trouble believing him. Fear prevented Ann from relaxing in the relationship. Larry did not deny his history of promiscuity. She did not deny her fear. They were both very honest. Larry wanted to be in control of the relationship. His lovemaking was often hurried, harsh, and unromantic. Ann did not enjoy it. Her fear exaggerated every act of his into meaning something other than what it did. Their sense of humor and openness helped them to push the past into the past. They became examples of GIVERS, and lovemaking became a loving act as it is meant to be. They did not settle for boring techniques to avoid passion.

GIVERS sometimes equate sex with Divine Love, part of the grand universal plan. This high regard for intimacy bonds the marriage in a special, almost holy manner. It is not taken for granted or left to the whims of chance.

Louise and Juan are a happily married couple. They survived stormy times because they were mutually interested in protecting the relationship. An open line of communication revealed Louise's many sexual taboos. Sex in the bedroom was acceptable, but anywhere else created guilt and discomfort. Juan understood her feelings and helped her to overcome them. The bedroom continued to be the setting for lovemaking, but foreplay was initiated in different rooms of the house. This loving and understanding approach allowed Louise to conquer her fear and aversion until eventually, the entire house became one huge erotic bedroom.

Juan felt uncomfortable in the nude. He was reared in a household full of sisters and was punished by his parents if he walked around not fully clothed. Louise had always been very proud of her body and had developed a healthy attitude toward it. Juan respected Louise's attitude and ideas. Seeking her help was both a joy and benefit. They both had lively imaginations that aided in reaching a solution. She discovered that he was comfortable with his nudity while in the shower. She began showering with him. Sexual enjoyment is, in part, a product of the imagination. Even when not together, Juan and Louise were able to create strong images of each other. Homecoming was always very special!

GIVERS are very patient and willing to seek resolutions to benefit the relationship rather than just self. They do not run from problems but tackle them as a team; working together with enthusiasm, a positive attitude and teamwork guarantees victory.

The Need for Change

Marge was really "stuck." She shared with the counselor how confused she was with the role of women in today's society. She was fifty years old, had been married for twenty-five years to the same man, and was frustrated with her inability to be a "modern woman."

Marge openly discussed many of her marital frustrations.

Marge: I've read a lot of books on improving relationships, but none of them seems to address my problem. I was raised in a very proper family. My father was the accepted head of the household, making all the major decisions for us. My mother was a lovely lady who was present, but made hardly any contribution to the conversation.

Therapist: How did this affect you?

Marge: I really think I got the idea that women should just accept things and keep smiling. You know, never rock the boat.

Therapist: What does that mean to you?

Marge: It means going along, especially when it involves sex.

Therapist: You sound angry when you say that.

Marge: I am. This is a new day. I can read. I can see how the world has changed. I think my husband would like me to be different in bed, but it is so difficult for me to just relax and let go.

Therapist: Let go of what?

Marge: All those old ideas of what I should and should not do or enjoy. I've honestly tried to change, but I end up angry and upset with my husband and myself.

Marge presents a clear picture of someone who has a strong program in her head dictating what a lady should or should not do. Such a program is difficult to blur and even harder to erase, but it is not impossible.

My advice to the women's club of America
is to raise more hell and few dahlias.
(William Allen White, 1868–1944)

A lady is one who never shows her underwear
unintentionally. (Lillian Day)

Being a GIVER will continue to be difficult for Marge in the area of sex unless she drops those old preconceived ideas and rules. Sex is part of love, and teaching is neither impossible nor inappropriate. Values are strongly implanted in all of us. The value of sex and everything that goes along with it had to be explored by the counselor and Marge.

Marge may or may not be able to change her strong value system. Her willingness to come to counseling certainly implies that she is at least making an attempt to change. The words that Marge negatively associates with sex were implanted in her subconscious as a child and not evaluated until the present. She has rearranged the words, but the fears surrounding them still persist.

Counseling or therapy was a unique experience, and she utilized it thoroughly. She even wrote down the times during the week that she felt guilt, fear, shame, or other relative emotions. She was not surprised at how they were usually linked to a sexual subject or innuendo.

Marge learned through hard work she could be a GIVER in a sexual sense. She also realized her value system did not have to be compromised. She gained confidence in making decisions based on information *now* instead of the *past*. Her old associations in her head gradually changed into disassociations. When she associated sex with guilt, she would relive the old experiences in her head with visualizations. She would actually go inside her head like watching a movie and would move into a disassociate state by evaluating her experiences from a different viewpoint.

A Final Word

Obviously, therapy will not necessarily cure a relationship of everything that is wrong. In cases where it is helpful, the degree differs from couple to couple. Success or failure is the ultimate responsibility of the couple. Genuine concern for the welfare of the relationship will invariably help to develop positive interaction. When the relationship is put first in each and every situation, it will not only survive, but also thrive, regardless of the circumstances. However, the importance of sexual communication cannot be overemphasized. Without it, the total communication network will suffer.

CHAPTER 5

Speaking from the Heart

L ove does not die. Difficult and unforgiving situations can impede love by encouraging it to die within the relationship, but its perpetual presence endures. Think of faltering love as once a beautiful lake left withered and dried up of drought. Although the lake itself has become dry, the water does not cease to exist. Also, adequate rainfall will replenish it as if the drought had never occurred.

Water is an irrepressible and perennial life force that manages to survive despite its natural enemies. The same is true of love. It can be driven so deeply into the crevices of the subconscious until it will appear to have dried up. If one were to dig deep enough beneath the surface, love would be rediscovered. Cruelty and unkindness dissipates love on the surface, forces it into the depths of rejection and denial, but it remains very much alive. It is an entity that exists in spite of us and dwells freely in the lives of the worthy and the willing. Love can be salvaged and fully restored, regardless of the present condition of the relationship.

Speaking from the Heart reveals thoughts of the real experts, *you*. The spontaneous and anonymous thoughts are overflowing with the kind of knowledge and wisdom that only living and observing life to its fullest can provide.

A random group was asked to respond to the following:

1. Please give me your definition of love and/or marriage.
2. Please define what a satisfying sexual/intimate relationship is to you.

The respondents in the first statement varied in ages from sixteen to forty, and in the second from twenty-three to forty. Both male and female, excluding the high school students, had varying educational backgrounds. Those who declined to participate complained the statements were either too vague or redundant and would have preferred a question that could have been answered by a yes or no.

The statements are purposely ambiguous. Understanding love in marriage and enjoying sex in intimacy remains a fascination for both the young and old. There is no right or wrong answer; each definition is personal and individualistic. A definitive answer is therefore not as clear-cut as defining what a green, yellow, or red light means.

Thus, the statements were presented as such to avoid fixed responses.

The responses from *you* support the idea that marriage is a mathematical contradiction—*one* plus *one* equals *one*. One respondent stated it quite eloquently: "Love can't be put in a nutshell or cleverly defined by Webster. If one pushed and a definition had to be given, I would define love simple as God. *God is love.* Marriage is the union of woman and man in God. Since God is love, without God, there could be no love in marriage. One ceases in marriage to be two and becomes one and is the whole in God."

The religious aspect of marriage is one that is shared by many.

"God loves us, so we should love one another."

"God forgives, so part of marriage is forgiving."

"Love and sex don't go together unless there is a religious bond."

"Spirit can be depended on and will help bring more true love in marriage."

"Commitment to something greater than each other will enhance love."

Understanding, commitment, sharing, and bonding were repeated themes. Understanding transcends egotism and dissension by recognizing them as insignificant. Commitment means a firm decision is made to follow through. It is proof of dedication and stick-to-itiveness. It is the fuel that energizes action. Sharing denotes the absence of extreme selfishness. Oftentimes, quality relationships are damaged from the lack of sharing. Sharing both the pleasant and unpleasant aspects of life actually nurtures the relationship and establishes a greater sense of trust. The fringe benefits of internalizing understanding, commitment, and sharing is the birth of bonding where two unique individuals began to merge into one being. The importance of communication was discussed only sparingly, which could correlate with the divorce statistics that suggest that 50–60 percent of all marriages end in divorce.

The lack of communication, although only a few emphasized its importance, is regarded as a major reason for divorce.

One young man stated, "I communicate better with my dogs than with my wife."

A female stated, "Love is turned off when we don't open our hearts to hearing and feeling each other's ideas."

An impressive number of virgins under the age of twenty-one willingly shared their ideas. Their thoughts on sex, love, and marriage had a similar theme.

"An intimate relationship for me so far has only been closeness in mind, a communication between two people, and a deep understanding."

"Marriage and love do not always go together."

"Marriage is trust and commitment, then sex will be good."

A general attitude of permissiveness, both in and out of marriage, seemed unacceptable for the most part.

"Sex with a lot of people does not go along with honesty and trust."

"Marriage is best when no other lovers are hanging around."

"Love grows between couples but goes away when one strays."

There were still a few who put the sex act first and love and marriage a weak second. "When I have sex, that is the most satisfying relationship to me. I don't have to care so long as I get what I want."

"Sex and love are not the same."

"I do not think one has to just have one partner."

"Marriage would be better if there was less emphasis on monogamy and more emphasis on having fun."

One respondent's ideas were particularly interesting in that they were quite different from the others. "Love is an emotion that is difficult to define precisely, partly because it has [or can have] numerous meanings. Love in the context of love felt toward a parent suggests an expected emotion because of genetic/physical ties. Love toward a friend is an enhanced emotional state because of closeness, bonding, or similarities. Love toward a lover/sexual partner indicates a deep emotional bond that transcends many aspects of life such as sexuality, physical closeness, openness, and unconditional acceptance.

"Marriage is a legalistic and patriarchal institution derived to keep women in their places [i.e., barefoot, pregnant, and in the kitchen]. It promotes a loss of identity for a woman as it suggests openly that her job is to fulfill his needs [e.g., love, honor, and obey] and requires her to keep the family together at all costs to avoid divorce of else suffer shame. Therefore, it promotes the superiority of the male.

"Sexual and intimate relationships are two entirely different concepts to me, though they could occur concurrently. Sexual relationships can be anywhere from incest, rape, an experimental encounter in the back of the Chevy on a Friday night, to a close, intimate relationship that includes sexual expression as part of it. My ideal sexual relationship is with a woman with whom I love a great deal, feel loved by her, can express my feelings to her without regard for being hurt in any capacity, and can coexist with her in an incredibly intimate manner. Furthermore, the relationship will be monogamous, but with no other restrictions/limitations placed on either partner. "Intimate relationships can, but do not have to, include a sexual component. To me, an intimate relationship is a relationship between two friends that involves openness to discuss personal and private things without fear of rejection, being made fun of, or criticism, etc. I feel like I have a number of intimate relationships. However, most are not now, nor will they ever be sexual in nature. They are purely a very close level of personal or emotional involvement with unconditional positive regard."

A Final Word

Sex is a component of lovemaking, but when indulged in the absence of love and commitment, it is simply an erotic act. Intimacy frequently involves lovemaking, but it can also mean the development of a very personal and wholesome relationship regardless of gender without violating the laws of nature. The full majestic beauty and the bottomless depth of love are abundantly discovered in relationships where commitment, understanding, and bonding play pivotal roles. The ability to utilize these qualities through well-developed communication skills greatly improves the success ratio in all aspects.

CHAPTER 6

Gender Myths

Men and women have traditionally been accused of possessing certain characteristic traits or idiosyncrasies solely on the basis of sex. Obviously there are physiological differences between males and females, but overall, people are simply people. While "there are some bad in the best of us and some good in the worst of us," neither sex has a monopoly on any particular trait, be it negative or positive.

One popular gender myth among men is that most women can be bought, while women believe most or all men are promiscuous. But there are promiscuous men and women. However, many men feel it's okay for them to cheat, but consider it whorish for women to do the same. Double standards are simply unacceptable in a genuine and loving relationship. Some women, if betrayed, will quickly say, "But I shared my body with him." Such a statement seems to suggest that while she shared her body with the man, he somehow did not share his body with her.

The words *prostitute* and *whore* are generally associated with individuals who market and sell themselves. Prostitution is a multifaceted term that is both controversial and emotional. A destitute parent with a sick child may resort to bartering to cover medical expenses. An unemployed wife may agree to have sex with her spouse as the only means of receiving financial support. The degree of severity or difficulty will vary in each situation, but there are several possible solutions to every problem. It is a matter of choice, and the inability to recognize other options is magnified by fear, shallow faith, and the lack of sound judgment in a critical situation. The secret, though not necessarily easy, is being able to select the best overall solution while under stress.

"The love of money is the root of all sorts of evil," and very few people are immune to its temptation. Many individuals will become very irate if offered fifty or a hundred dollars to sleep with someone. If the ante were continually raised, many will eventually succumb. Arguably, almost everyone can be bought, but different people simply have different prices, and the price is not always necessarily money. If you cannot be bought one way or the other, congratulations for you are indeed an admirable exception to the rule. However, the statement "everyone can be bought" by no means implies everyone is immoral. But it does suggest that most of us, under unbearable conditions or circumstances, will likely make decisions that are unimaginable to us now. Moreover, everyone tends to justify his or her actions, be they good or bad. And when most of us explain our situations, we are either the victim or the hero. The overall point is that much of what we take for granted as being uniquely male or female are simply myths, quirks, and vicious lies that have been perpetrated via secondhand or three-thousand-hand information.

Almost daily you will hear someone say, "All men are like that." *All* is quite inappropriate. The following are common myths, some more applicable to one gender than the other. As you read them, you will probably think of some favorites of yours that could have very easily been included.

1. All men think with their sex organs.
2. All women are superficial.
3. All men have more than one woman.
4. All women are out for money.
5. All men are inconsiderate.
6. All women are vindictive.
7. All men are insensitive.
8. All women use their bodies for negotiation.
9. All men are out for sex.
10. All women are domineering.
11. All men are unromantic.
12. All women are too emotional.
13. All men are mama's babies.
14. All women are stuck on themselves.
15. All men are stingy.

16. All women are teasers.
17. All men are pushy and aggressive.
18. All men are liars.

A Final Word

Many individuals may or may not be guilty of the preceding myths. But those who are will be both men and women, but not *all!* The ultimate fact, however, is that some myths will eventually become larger than life. Keep in mind that the same word, idea, or thought spoken from the mouth of a liar can be the truth spoken by another. Words are simply a tool to communicate an idea and not the idea itself. Use them wisely, concentrate on being the very best you can be, and you will appreciate and be appreciated by spouse, family, and friends.

Part II

THE SOLUTION

PRELUDE TO PART II

U p to this point, part I has dealt primarily with identification and discussion of the GIVER and TAKER. Part II offers suggestions and/ or exercises that are of extreme benefit to everyone interested in loving and being loved. Although not entirely an easy task, it challenges you to keep that initial mystique and intrigue of the relationship alive. Style is as important as substance; therefore, do not take each other for granted. Treat each day as a big event or production that only your together-ness could have produced.

The following fourteen topic areas do not automatically guarantee success, but if faithfully practiced, they will produce change. Remember that neither success nor failure is the result of a single action, and nor is the result necessarily evident when the act is committed. Consider the lack of evidence at the very moment that a child is conceived. It takes time for the pregnancy to become evident. In that these tools may be new to you, remember that they must be used consistently and faithfully in order to change or improve your life.

1. **Use of Imagination** is a reminder that it is a gift that is only limited by lack of development. The first step toward solving any obstacle is use of the imagination.

2. **Surprise** is an effective contraceptive to prevent boredom.

3. **The Emperor's New Clothes** is a reminder that honesty must not take a back seat in the communication process.

4. **Respect Feelings** encourages fair play and growth because words sometimes get in the way.

5. **Allow Change** is very important because an inevitable constant in life is the flux of change.

6. **Silence Is Golden** is as tantamount to communicating as verbalizing. Contrary to popular belief, some thoughts must be properly digested before they can be regurgitated and shared in a comprehensible and effective manner.

7. When logic and reason fail, remember, **Man and Woman** share a bond that exceeds the realms of understanding.

8. **Leisure Time Sharing** challenges the reader to get away from the norm of day-to-day living and share the fringe benefits of togetherness and spontaneity.

9. **Spiritual Enrichment** emphasizes the importance of involving the Creator of the Universe in the affairs of the heart.

10. Nothing, absolutely nothing, is accomplished without **Education** to include a successful relationship; therefore, education is a must if marriage is to be given a fair chance for survival.

11. **Physical Health and Exercise** is necessary in order to maintain harmony with the mental, physical, and spiritual, the mind, body, and soul.

12. **Contemplation** is a mental hotline that allows self to get in touch with self.

13. **Humor** helps to balance the victories and defeats.

14. **The Video Mind** records the unfolding of life as it is being played by each of us on the stage of life.

These topics are the final chapters, and while nothing works absolutely every time for everyone, they are essential tools necessary to strengthen love during otherwise fragile times.

CHAPTER 7

Use of Imagination

The imagination is the birthplace of creative ideas and timely inventions. It has the creative ability to escape circumstances and to visualize a situation not as it is but as it can be. When it comes to love, the GIVER understands the importance of using the imagination. The TAKER, once motivated by the desire to improve the relationship, can learn this art that will eventually loosen the tight reins bridling their hearts and emotions.

Prod your imagination by selecting a book to read that provokes a childlike state. Read the story or poem slowly, look carefully at the pictures, and imagine yourself as being part of it. A book of nursery rhymes or Aesop's fables is an excellent selection. Once the skill is mastered, enhance the imagination further by reading passages from other books. After reading a passage, the individual should once again put self in the story. Instead of children's stories, choose excerpts or short stories involving love. This exercise may take days or weeks, but it should be practiced for at least fifteen minutes per day. The read material should be uplifting or either evokes feelings of love or a childlike receptive state.

When it is determined by the TAKER that the imagination is developed to the point of placing self in the story, take another step by integrating the spouse/partner into it. The TAKER should clearly visualize his partner in a loving situation.

During other times of the day, use the imagination to send feelings of goodwill and love. Scan magazines or ads, view the pleasant pictures, and try replacing the model's face with your partner's. Soon this habit will become a spontaneous act that will help to subconsciously change the TAKER's view of his or her partner. It takes practice!

CHAPTER 8

Surprise

GIVERS and TAKERS, at some point, begin to act in a predictable manner. If the predictable pattern is reversed, the situation automatically changes. Couples can reverse roles by taking turns planning vacations or long weekends. Even dinner engagements can be planned in this manner. The individual doing the planning should reveal only the date, time of departure, and what to wear and bring. Another element of surprise can be a personal, handwritten note sent in the mail expressing gratitude for a nice evening. Genuine warmth is felt from reading a love note or message that comes from the heart of the sender. Spontaneous joy felt from these activities brings newness and excitement to the marriage.

"Variety" within the relationship "is the spice of life." Although unplanned sex has aphrodisiac qualities, planned time for sex can also be a pleasant surprise. Accentuate the stage with soft candlelight, seductive music, aromatic fragrance, and a romantic setting away from home. Even the hardened TAKER is touched by the element of surprise. A wife who had not shared a decent conversation with her husband in months initiated an evening in the bathroom. They bathed, had dinner by candlelight, shared sexual intimacies, and even slept on a bedroll in the bathroom. Nothing within the bounds of chaste behavior is too far out if used to improve a relationship! Adding new pieces to the wardrobe or trying a new hairstyle is a good primer, but remember, just one simple event seldom helps the relationship, but rather many little ones!

CHAPTER 9

"The Emperor's New Clothes"

Remember the story of the *Emperor's New Clothes*? Everyone was afraid to tell him that he was not wearing any clothes. An innocent child who was not afraid to be honest finally informed the emperor that he was naked. Games or exercises similar in nature to this story are often played in marriage. The husband may despise the opera, for example, but pretends to love it and chooses not to openly discuss it, only to develop bitter discontentment. But it is better to discuss the situation and negotiate a settlement rather than harbor negative feelings.

If some action or nonaction needs to be changed, it needs to be addressed. Enter into negotiation or the problem-solving process with the blind determination of the childlike mind. It is always open to new ideas and does not fear the rejection of old ones.

THE MORE CLEARLY WE EXPERIENCE
SOMETHING AS NONSENSE, THE MORE
CLEARLY WE ARE EXPERIENCING THE
BOUNDARIES OF OUR OWN SELF-
IMPOSED COGNITIVE STRUCTURES.
NONSENSE IS THAT WHICH DOES NOT
FIT INTO THE PREARRANGED PATTERNS
WHICH WE HAVE SUPERIMPOSED ON
REALITY. THEREE IS NO SUCH THING AS
NONSENSE APART FROM A JUDMENTAL
INTELLECT WHICH CALLS IT THAT.
(Gary Zukav, *The Dancing Wu Li Masters*)

CHAPTER 10

Respect Feelings

Feelings are genuine, private, and an important part of our being. Respect of those feelings is a difficult task to learn because we tend to want others to feel the way we do. We must never deny the partner the right to feel any way he or she wants to feel. It is natural for our feelings to fluctuate from positive to negative. Each of us has the right to have inconsistent feelings. Never say, "You shouldn't feel that way." If someone is angry, that should be respected and intelligently discussed.

A relationship is never improved by dictating how one should feel. Our biases should not be superimposed on anyone else. They often surface and create a strong judgmental attitude before the other person has a chance to fully express self. Mindreading is not likely, yet it is attempted in most long-term relationships. "I know what you are thinking," "I know how you feel about that," or "I know you didn't like that." These are just a few phrases often expressed to a marital counselor.

Individuals who exhibit eccentric and exaggerated behavior make overcoming such biases very exhausting, but overcoming them is a must for the survival of the relationship. Each of us has the right to be different and should be allowed to do so. The habit of asking questions and learning from those differences can be developed. "How do you feel about that?" "Is that the way you feel?" "Are your feelings different from mine?" These are questions that keep the doors of communication open.

The TAKER often forgets that the individual's freedom to feel is as important as the freedom to start a new job, have a hobby, or to participate in other activities. We can only have freedom in any area of our lives if we allow others to have it. To receive love, you must first love, and to have freedom, you must be willing to grant it. It is difficult to let someone just be, but it is necessary for transformation.

CHAPTER 11

Allow Change

There are many more reasons to change than there are to remain the same. A few of life's experiences that changes us are sickness, changes in marital status, self-esteem, new friends or loves, jobs, death, religious experiences, new hobbies, counseling, or simply living. Many names are given the changes that takes place in our lives— midlife crisis, growing up, going through a phase, being reborn, starting again, regressing, going off the deep end, and showing the real self. Change is not always allowed in a healthy marriage, but it is expected and appreciated. We want people to stay in their assigned roles so we do not have to think too much about their behavior or ours.

To varying degrees, the fear of change lurks in the background of all married couples. A newborn baby in the family demands a tremendous change on the part of the parents. This change seems to carry with it a load of frustration and guilt. After all, are not children supposed to bring joy and happiness? Young couples have to be encouraged to keep their sense of humor and to spend cozy private time together. The TAKER has a particularly difficult time accepting this change because a baby is someone who can hardly be yelled at; therefore, the TAKER resorts to being nasty toward the spouse.

Older couples receiving therapy cite "too much change in attitude" as their number one need for help. The aging process increases one's philosophical approach to life and diminishes the need for physical activity. Certainly this is not a hard and fast rule, but it is a natural one. It is a change that both try to avoid, and in many cases, the result is resentment and bitterness.

Change is a part of life that travels with time. It arrives on schedule and can be exciting and challenging if not viewed as the enemy.

CHAPTER 12

Silence Is Golden

Traffic jams, shrieking and offensive voices, the noise of jets circling the city, and other industrial and environmental sounds can bombard the senses. Couples sometimes compound these sounds by developing the habit of talking a lot without really saying anything. Low self-esteem and a lack of positive interaction can also contribute to constant chatter. Quiet walks with periodic stops to just listen have tremendous benefits.

Kramer and Lee had resorted to a vicious contest to see who could be the most effective TAKER. The pain of everyday conversation and activity had become a dreaded affair. They recognized the fact that the marriage had become unbearable and were willing to try and change. Their jobs permitted them to get off work early in the evenings so they could spend time together. The first improvement was their ability to listen to one another. After a while, the power of silence was recognized and appreciated.

The silent treatment worked for them. Once a day they went walking in the woods for at least an hour. They were told not to say anything but just to observe, listen, and smell. The walk was deliberately slow, and they were instructed to stop every five minutes, pick up an object, and examine it by smell or touch, and to simply listen to both the human silence and the sounds of nature at the same time.

Other couples have utilized this method by walking down a street or in a park. One couple used to go to the zoo or museum. They would concentrate on paintings and sit and marvel at the silence that surrounded them.

Silence is the element in which great things fashion themselves. (Thomas Carlyle, *Sartor Resartus*)

Once couples become comfortable with silence, a deeper level of communication has developed.

CHAPTER 13

Man and Woman

Is there an understanding of the female and male relationship that goes much deeper than personality? Do we learn from each other in a profound spiritual way that exceeds the spoken word? One school of thought is that the male and female is totally different kinds of energy. Both need the other for survival on this planet. The male, being the aggressor, uses his energy to keep us moving forward. The female, the softer and more empathic of the two, uses her energy to balance the aggression of the male. There are many other theories that are worth exploring. Couples who are afraid to explore their own philosophy on the subject are usually the ones who are reluctant to explore other areas of life.

Certainly the role of the male and female is merging. Is this suitable for everyone? A strong belief system concerning the roles of both can be evaluated and even changed if necessary. The repression of females in the past has improved after a long and arduous fight. This transition has encouraged women to be assertive when it is appropriate to the situation. It could mean taking a gentleman out to lunch or simply tossing aside the many outdated stigmata.

How is this change affecting the marital role? The male and female might decide to change roles to accomplish a mutual goal. Man is no longer ridiculed if he stays home and enjoys the role of homemaker, nor is woman ridiculed for desiring to be an executive. The sharing of housework, yard work, or the rearing of the children is now an acceptable joint responsibility. Old prejudices are being pushed aside for new solutions.

CHAPTER 14

Leisure Time Sharing

An important secret to developing, maintaining, and strengthening a relationship is to spend quality time together. The habit of becoming playmates for the weekend or even for a few hours has incalculable benefits. It is easy to descend into the emotions surrounding the hustle and bustle of life and become too anxious or preoccupied to interact in a positive and nurturing manner.

Daily stressors are unavoidable. Every opportunity should be taken to lighten the stress. Leisure time sharing and playfulness encourages laughter and joyful expression. Laughter massages the inner person in the same way that a hot tub bath relaxes the body.

Many negative experiences and emotions such as anger, hatred, jealousy, or anxiety incite an individual to kick into emotional overdrive. If this state persists, the wear and tear has far-reaching consequences on mind, body, and soul. Remember what will happen if the passing gear of your automobile is permanently engaged? Each individual has a tension threshold. If constantly "hyped up" or agitated, the emotional passing gear remains engaged. The result is often an emotional breakdown or illness.

The TAKER is frequently engulfed by negative emotions. The unreasonable demands and the *me-first syndrome* becomes a source of frustration in the relationship.

There are many fringe benefits of playtime. The simple act of relaxation can open the heart of the TAKER to the ideas of love. The compassion of the GIVER and a supportive environment can be a catalyst for change.

CHAPTER 15

Spiritual Enrichment

History is a chronicle of man's plight for fulfillment. He has progressively moved through the vacuum of time, hurdling the unknown and winning against impossible odds. Man carved the wheel from stone—a remarkable step in the direction of progress. He moved from animal to mechanical transportation, from ground to air to space travel. Man has the remarkable ability to solve the seemingly unsolvable and to conquer the unconquerable. A cure for the AIDS epidemic and COVID-19 will be found, just as a cure or vaccine has been found for most diseases.

Man is the conqueror of disease, space, industry, transportation, and education. But the inability to develop the capacity to love God, family, neighbor, countryman, and ultimately self is the only area that consistently eludes us. War among nations is the fruit of mankind's inability to truly love one another. Every religion has attempted to make the concept of love a foundation for its teaching. The lack of love disguises itself in hate, anger, and confusion of purpose.

The spiritual enrichment of a couple can be accomplished in many ways. Many spend time alone in prayer or contemplation, and others attend services at a particular church or building. The purpose of worship is to teach the concept of love and to make it a strong element in our consciousness on a daily basis.

Our lives are a reflection of thoughts. Alexander Cannon remarked in his book, *Powers That Be*, "A thought sooner or later becomes a thing. Your thoughts are a constant prayer to, or rejection of God." Meditation, contemplation, and prayer can tap into solutions that are not totally influenced by the power of the mind, solutions that are intuitive, creative, and loving.

SPIRITUAL ENRICHMENT IS NOT SOMETHINE YOU DO TO ENHANCE YOUR LIFE, IT IS YOUR LIFE AND YOUR ONLY REAL MEANS OF GOVERING SELF. THE POWER OF YOU GROWS AND APPEARS IN THE FORM OF **LOVE.** (Cameron Fox)

CHAPTER 16

Education

The most difficult task is achieved only after consistent practice. Practice does not necessarily make perfect, but the desire for perfect or uncompromised practice makes perfect or ensures growth and maturity. Doctors and lawyers do not become professionals by the act of wanting. Their desire was coupled with education.

Would you travel on an airplane piloted by someone who wanted to be a pilot? Or allow an individual who wanted to be a doctor to operate on you? Learning by trial and error is not acceptable in many endeavors and occupations. The skills necessary to achieve success in any given area are developed through education and hard work.

Education before the fact can often prevent incompatible or unloving individuals from marrying. It can reveal motives, goals, and personality quirks. Education, in the form of counseling, encourages each person to learn how to lovingly and agreeably disagree. It teaches couples how to argue in a manner that produces loving conclusions and solutions.

Communication techniques (e.g., good listening skills and the ability to lovingly and agreeably disagree) can, with constant practice, afford a couple a clearer understanding of a given situation. The hidden messages may have been misinterpreted. Education uncovers them and allows the couple to view them in the presence of a counselor, thus reducing the emotional content of words.

Money, like sex, can be an ever-present source of discontentment. Problems with finances often uncover fears that relate to childhood experiences. Education can assist in the process that will change those things. The skill and tact learned through education will nurture the roots of love.

CHAPTER 17

Physical Health and Exercise

Physical health awareness has taken on a significant role in the lives of many conscientious individuals. In order to look good, one must feel good. Think of the mind and body as the engine and transmission in your car. One is of little use without the other. Both must be kept in good operating condition to ensure reliable transportation.

Stewart and Diane's marriage suffered when he succumbed to the temptations of food and became obese. If she had wanted a fat and slovenly mate, she would have married one in the first place! His overall deterioration in appearance was difficult for her to accept. Other men were beginning to look more and more attractive to her. Physical exercise and education solved their problem, but it took time and patience. Poor health maintenance is one of many reasons for widespread infidelity.

While engaging in physical activity, one can interact with another on a level that is refreshing and tension-free. In that problems are inevitable, it is often easier to end a dispute or war off the battlefield than to have won on it. Taking the problems out of the household away from their battlefield can be very effective. A neutral ground is an effective place for negotiation. Jogging or other outdoor exercises offers a neutral territory.

Physical exercise improves self-esteem and self-confidence. If we are self-conscious about our appearances, we tend to be less willing to develop and maintain a healthy and intimate relationship. Bodies certainly do not have to be perfect for one to enjoy a healthy relationship, but feeling good about self is a definite plus.

CHAPTER 18

Contemplation

Contemplation is a way to bring out the real *you* from the woodwork of the subconscious. It is a form of pure thought exercise that reveals the true nature of things. Couples who allocate time for this endeavor develop skills to sort out problems, find solutions, and subsequently free themselves to focus on the important concepts of love.

It is easy for the thinking process to become fogged. Situations become unclear, and a cobweb of confusion and prejudiced information reigns supreme. Going within self with meditation or contemplation allows the internal world of self to emerge. The quiet and stillness of contemplation does not require a particular body posture, but it does require a receptive attitude. As one sits or lies in stillness, thoughts are simply observed while the mind remains open and humble.

One teacher encourages couples to focus on the breathing process while observing the arrival and departure of thought. The inhaling process is considered progress, the exhaling as retrogression, and the pause in between as rejuvenation. The breathing process captures the unique pattern of life.

Some have found it helpful to take a phrase from a book of poetry, something that is positive, and to read it, absorb it, and to relax and simply live life as it unfolds. A group of TAKERS learned to sit quietly and listen. They listened for the sound that was the farthest away, such as a faraway train or plane, and moved to the second closest sound and proceeded to move closer and closer until they discovered an inner sound. The results were so amazing that they continued this exercise long after therapy was completed.

The ability to change is very important in a relationship. Contemplation develops awareness and helps us welcome change. Remember, "Progress, growth and change are the order of life, and the only thing that is constant is the reality of change" (Paul J. Meyer). Once our inside world is changed, the outside world will then be perceived in a uniquely different manner.

GIVERS VERSUS TAKERS

AS WE CLIMB UP THE LADDER OF LIFE,
WE SOMETIMES FALL DOWN, AND
AT OTHER TIMES WE SIMPLY HOLD
ON. REALIZING THIS PATTERN WILL
STRENGTHEN YOU NOT TO PANIC WHEN
LIFE IS NOT PROGRESSING AS EXPECTED.
NIGHT IS FOLLOWED BY DAY AND THERE
IS DUSK AND DAWN IN-BETWEEN.
(Rufus Rawls)

CHAPTER 19

Humor

Humor is important to health maintenance. It also plays a check-and-balance role in a relationship. It allows us to take life seriously and yet enjoy the lighter side of it. Life's demands often put the full-court press on us if the proper proactive defense has not been developed. It is virtually impossible to genuinely smile and remain unhappy at the same time. The inner being smiles with the outer.

Television has skillfully used humor as a means of dealing with sensitive and controversial issues. Humor disarms hostility and prejudice to such a degree that both the irony and less serious aspects of a situation can be viewed with an open and objective mind. We allow the small problems in life to become insurmountable obstacles if the importance of humor is not integrated into the total health maintenance program.

"No living creature can laugh except man." This quote by Og Mandino captures the importance of laughter. The use of positive and loving humor can help reduce uncomfortable emotions. Instead of bickering and fighting over what is wrong or lacking in a relationship, focus on what is good and right in it. The negotiation process on any level, conducted in the presence of a smiling face and a jovial heart, makes the task of finding agreeable solutions to a problem much easier. When confronted with adversity, the wise person remembers that everything on this planet changes with regularity. Sometimes the mere act of just hanging on helps to solve problems.

It takes less energy to protect the relationship using humor than drawing swords and fighting. Love, affection, and genuine intimacy are difficult to revive without many long hours of effort. Humor applied properly will neutralize seemingly large obstacles and reduce them to their actual size.

CHAPTER 20

The Video Mind

A popular family pastime is renting videos or movies and enjoying the excitement of watching one's favorite stars in the home. Sometimes it is a dramatic film accompanied by emotional outbursts, or it may be a comedy, mystery, or a travelogue. Rarely do we watch a movie more than once unless it is particularly outstanding. Most of the time the movies rented before the latest technology was placed in the plastic case and returned to the video store.

In any event, the mind functions like a video camera. It is forever taking pictures and recording feelings that can be played and replayed whenever desired. Intensely emotional tapes or mental recordings create a rush of excitement. If one tolerates a large portion of dullness in life, the old tapes may be replayed more frequently. Examples of unpleasant experiences that the video mind may record are

Rotten Vacation, Argument on the Plane, the Time He Hurt My Feelings, and many others. Tragedies such as combat experiences or death of loved ones are also big favorites to play over and over.

In that the workings of the video mind can be difficult to understand, taking a psychology course, reading self-help books, and participating in other activities to develop self is a good habit to adopt. By becoming more aware of the intricate workings of the brain, couples can discover methods to protect the relationship against the ever-present probability of failure.

TO HAVE AND TO HOLD FROM THIS DAY FORWARD, FOR BETTER, FOR WORSE, FOR RICHER, FOR POORER, IN SICKNESS, AND IN HEALTH, TO LOVE AND TO CHERISH TILL DEATH DO US PART.
(*Book of Common Prayer*)

CHAPTER 21

How to Recognize a Taker

Marriage is not an exact science. In other words, there is not a full-proof method that guarantees you will not marry or become seriously involved with a TAKER. Most impostors can fake it so long as the relationship remains superficial. Love, lust, or other ulterior motives can cause you to become "legally blind" to the TAKER's faults. However, if marriage is approached objectively, yet romantically and with sound judgment, there are telltale signs that will identify the TAKER. Your individual ability or awareness to recognize a TAKER will depend on several factors: you not being swept away by an emotional tidal wave, not being gullible to a smooth line, and not being so naïve that you fall prey to a cunning individual.

Allow your potential love mate the opportunity to talk about whatever he or she chooses. In fact, encourage it! Subject matter is not as important as the process itself. Each of us has basic interests that include a fulfilling relationship, career, and a relationship with out Creator, whatever we perceive Him to be.

Listen and ask questions that stimulate conversation, and quite a bit of what you need to know will be voluntarily shared. The information may be clear and concise, or it may be cryptic and need deciphering. Pay equal attention to both verbal and nonverbal facets of the conversation. The words *I* and *me* are frequently used in their conversation. In fact, the usage of these words may very well become trite or overused.

Be sure to ask questions about previous relationship(s). Take heed if all the blame is consistently placed on the other person. A TAKER is inclined to blame the "other person" and will frequently reflect only on the negative aspects of the relationship. A GIVER will have fond memories that will be punctuated by a sparkle in the eye or a painted smile across the lips.

However, after reading this book, if you find that you are already married to a TAKER or are a TAKER yourself, use the suggestions in this book to facilitate change. If it is your partner who is the TAKER, ask him or her to read *Givers versus Takers* and let you know if it is as good as your friend says it is. After which, the two of you can discuss it. The point is you do not want to suggest the reading of it because he or she is a terrible person and needs to change. Many creative approaches can be used to accomplish this end. Regardless of the approach, be sure to use tact and creativity. If you are the TAKER, ask your mate to share the reading experience with you and to discuss the various aspects of the book.

Remember, change is not that difficult once the decision to change and a reason for change has been recognized.

CHAPTER 22

Final Words

Marriage is a wondrous journey into unchartered, often potentially dangerous territory where at least 50 percent of its voyagers return divorced, suffering unspeakable pain, and often marred for life. These couples were either in love or shared strong emotional ties when they married. Thus an appropriate question is, What went wrong following the "I do" and between the honeymoon and the arguments or fights that led to divorce? The reasons are obviously many, to include the likelihood that far too few couples actually commit to the marriage vows during or following the ceremony, despite their ritualistic consensus. The marital commitment is not just a matter of going through the motions during the ceremony but actually living up to them, both the good and bad times following the wedding.

Givers versus Takers is a necessary road map, if you will, for any voyager who is committed to making marriage a blissful journey and not a divorce-bound destination. This road map stresses the importance of packing the proper baggage for the journey. An uncompromising willingness to effective communicate is a must. Marital journeys are often aborted or crashed because the importance of minute-to-minute communication is ignored or underestimated.

Do not try to reshape or change your mate into what you perceive as ideal or perfect. Imperfection is a human frailty. It is unrealistic to believe you can force your mate to change, that you can mold or reshape him or her to meet your expectations. Regard your differences in a positive and creative way. Remember, true love is a student of awareness. It is always seeking ways to improve the relationship by seeking the ideal of perfection through continuous growth. In other words, each couple has the propensity to become a fine-tuned, synchronous unit.

Change can be forged but not forced. One dictionary describes *forge* as "to move forward steadily, as if against difficulties." Couples should marry with the intent and desire to help each other to become the very best person that they can, but should not try to make each other over. A TAKER's true personality cannot be forced into compatibility with that of a GIVER.

Irrespective of differences, the importance of protecting the relationship and preserving the concept of love must be placed on a pedestal. Take Marge, for example, in chapter 3, who recognized her preconditioned ideas about sex, but who was willing to grow past them. And Larry and Susan, who were able to recognize and resolve why they desired separate vacations.

Do not become overwhelmed or normalized by boredom. Love enjoys being romanced, and romance loves the surprise of spontaneity. Let each day in our lives be an unwritten and unchartered adventure. In other words, do not have a script that says you must watch or not watch television every evening, for example. Do not submit to a routine way of doing whatever it is that you do together the exact same way each and every time. Enjoy being in control by writing your own script to your lives.

Be thankful if you are already a GIVER, but do not despair if you are a TAKER. The beauty of life is that we have within our power the ability to change. The impact that this book will have on your life will not exceed your willingness to change or your desire to use the information herein. Keep in mind that the breakdown in a relationship is seldom the fault of just one individual. Admittedly, one will clearly be more the blame than the other, but both are ultimately at fault. If the intent is to save the relationship, energy should be devoted not to blaming anyone but to saving the relationship.

Do not succumb to the temptation to abandon your present mate for someone else, although this is unfortunately sometimes the result. There is no guarantee that the problems you now have will not be part of the new relationship. Remember, you are going to follow you. Wherever you go, you will be there when you get there because you will take you there. If changing relationships becomes your method of dealing with problems that arise—and they most certainly will—you are destined to relationship hopping for the rest of your life. Concentrate on victory, make it a concept or creed to follow, and strive not to entertain divorce as the only solution when the going gets tough. After all, marriage is a commitment meant to end only in death. However, "the death of the moth is the birth of the butterfly." Marriage, particularly from the biblical perspective, is a commitment that only death should terminate. However, two very important points should be considered. First of all, statistics show that approximately 50 percent of all marriages do, in fact, end in divorce. Second, the death of marriage does not necessarily mean that either partner has died physically, mentally, or spiritually.

In regard to the first point, a balance between idealism and realism must be derived in order to understand that there will always remain an inherent flaw within the institution of marriage on the part of humanity. Ideally, each of us marries with the desire, whether spoken or unspoken, for that marriage to last a lifetime. However, the realistic probability of that happening in each and every marriage is totally unrealistic. Different people with varying expectations enter into marriage for different reasons. However, to remain married simply for the sake of being married, while being deprived of the joys and needs sought from that marriage in the first place, is simply asking perhaps too much.

Marriage, due to lack of commitment or understanding, for example, can deteriorate to such an irreversible degree that all love and a sense of belonging can die out. As a result, the relationship is, for all practical purposes, dead. Therefore, as unfortunate as it is, divorce sometimes becomes the lesser of the two evils. Therefore the statement "until death do us part" can literally mean, and often does, death as in the loss of physical life. It can also mean the death of the relationship via the death of love, understanding, commitment, communication, respect, mutual interest, trust, and the desire to live together. All of which can end the relationship or marriage as emphatically as physical death does. However, a dead relationship can, in many cases, be revived if both parties are aware of what is killing it and are committed to administering love resuscitation to the relationship. It is not necessary to remain yoked to a miserably failing or seemingly dead marriage. God specializes in resurrecting things, people, and situations that are dead!

But insofar as divorce is concerned, it was never a part of God's divine plan for humanity. In Matthew 19:8, Jesus said, *"Moses because of the hardness of your hearts suffered you to put away your wives: but from the beginning it was not so."* Some mates, then and now, were using all types of flimsy and ungodly reasons for divorce. But Jesus gave one exception to the "until death do us part" intention of God, and that is fornication, to include all types of sexual sins, such as adultery, homosexuality, and bestiality. However, due to the hardness of the hearts, the death of some marriages precedes the death of the couple. Nonetheless, please do not forget to remember: God specializes in resurrecting the dead. If you are willing to invite God in and are willing to obey His instruction, He will revive, restore, and rejuvenate your marriage.

I pray your reading experience was inspiring and enlightening!

ACKNOWLEDGMENTS

I n retrospect, we recognize the need to thank everyone we have met who touched our lives in a special way. Your support, or the lack of, gave us the stick-to-itiveness that made this book a reality. Closer to home, however, we are deeply indebted and eternally grateful to our spouses, John and Ora. "Without your assistance and support, we would have long ago abandoned this project." The encouragement and inspiration that Angelique Rawls has always provided her father is deeply appreciated.

Words do not render themselves sufficient in expressing our immeasurable thanks to doctors Judith Lyons, Tom Payne, and Phil Godding. Dr. Lyons's technical assistance and untiring patience is beyond measure. "Without you, we would not have found our way through the jungle of words and composition." Doctors Payne and Godding's knowledge of computers rescued us from remaining lost someplace between starting and finishing this book.

Finally, this book was written more than two decades ago, but the latest statistics on divorce and children born out of wedlock was not included within the pages you have read. Inclusion of the most recent statistics available will have only sub-stantiated the fact that the institution of marriage continues to be disproportionately under attack. And although many changes have taken place in our society and the family since *Givers versus Takers* was originally written, the most important point of this book remains unchanged: regardless of anything and everything else, communication is the single most important attribute of marriage, a truth emphasized and reemphasized throughout this book. Therefore the relevancy of this book is exceedingly timelier now than ever.

Thanks again!

BIBLIOGRAPHY

Bandler, Richard. *Using Your Brain for a Change.* Moab: Real People Press, 1985.

Bloomfield, Harold H. *Making Peace with Yourself.* New York: Ballantine Books, 1985.

Bry, Adelaide. *How to Get Angry without Feeling Guilty.* New York: Signet Classics, 1976.

Byrne, Robert. *The Other 637 Best Things Anybody Ever Said.* New York, Fawcett Crest, 1984.

Buscaglia, Leo F. *Personhood.* New York: Fawcett-Columbine Publications, 1982.

Cannon, Alexander. *Powers That Be.* New York: E. P. Dutton & Co., Inc., 1935.

Card, Orson Scott. *Characters & Viewpoint.* Cincinnati: Writer's Digest Books, 1988.

Davidoff, Henry, ed. *The Pocket Book of Quotations,* New York: Pocket Books, 1952.

Dunn, David. *Try Giving Yourself Away.* Englewood Cliffs: Prentice Hall, Inc., 1970.

Evatt, Chris and Bruce Feld. *The Givers and Takers.* New York, MacMillan, 1983.

Frankl, Viktor. *The Unheard Cry for Meaning.* New York: Washington Square Press, 1978.

Fromm, Erich. *The Art of Loving.* New York: Harper & Row, 1956.

Lair, Jess. *I Ain't Much Baby but I'm All I've Got.* New York: Fawcett Publications, 1972.

Lao Tzu. *Tao Te Ching.* Translated by Gia-Fu Feng and Jane English. New York: Random House, 1972.

Lowery, Katherine. "The Ten Commandments of Love." *Mademoiselle Magazine* (September 1985).

Mandino, Og. *The Greatest Salesman in the World.* Hollywood, Florida: Frederick Fell Publishers, Inc.

Meyer, Paul J. Success Motivation Institute. Texas, 1984.

Morgan, James, ed. *Love Is Now (The Moods of Love).* Kansas City: Hallmark Crown Editions, 1971.

New American Standard Bible. W. T. B. Press, Inc.

Pocs, Ollie, ed. *Marriage and Family 88/89.* Guilford: Dushkin Publishing Group, Inc., 1988.

Robbins, Anthony. *Unlimited Power.* Fawcett-Columbine Publications, 1987.

Smoyak, Shirley, RN, PhD. *The Psychiatric Nurse as a Family Therapist.* New York: John Wiley & Sons, Inc., 1975.

Twitchell, Paul. *The Flute of God.* Minneapolis: Eckankar, 1969.

Viscott, David, MD. *The Language of Feelings.* New York: Pocket Books, 1976.

Weinberg, George. *The Heart of Psychotherapy.* New York: St. Martin's Press, 1984.

Wing, R. L. *The Art of Strategy.* New York: Doubleday, 1988.

Woolf, Henry Bosley, ed. *Merriam-Webster Dictionary.* New York: Pocket Books, 1974.

Zukav, Gary. *The Dancing Wu Li Masters.* New York: William Morrow & Co., Inc., 1979.

ABOUT THE AUTHORS

Cameron lives on a farm in Clinton, Mississippi, with her husband, John a local attorney. She has four grown children and four grandchildren. She presently works at the Jackson VA Medical Center, Jackson, Mississippi, as a therapist and educator. She has worked in the field of psychiatry since 1973, but as a registered nurse and counselor, and group therapy is an additional skill. She conducts biweekly groups for Vietnam Veterans and veterans of World War II and the Korean conflict. She also works privately with a group, Clinical Counseling Associates.

Recent lectures given by Cameron to medical personnel include the following: "Dealing with Difficult People," "You and Emotion," "Dreams—a Method of Problem Solving," "When the Caregiver Needs Help," "Stress—How to Cope," and "Negotiation."

She has many hobbies, including horseback riding, traveling, and oil painting.

* * *

Rufus lives in Jackson, Mississippi, with his wife Ora, who is a procurement manager. He is the father of three children. He is presently employed at the Jackson VA Medical Center in Jackson, Mississippi. As a rehabilitation technician in psychology services, he works with psychiatrically impaired veterans and families. He is also involved in research on psychological adjustment and coping with traumatic events. As a distributor for Success Motivation Institute (SMI), he conducted modification behavioral and motivational seminars.

He has many interests, which include horseback riding, drawing, and meditating.

Footnote: The information about the authors is applicable to when this book was originally written.